Clothes

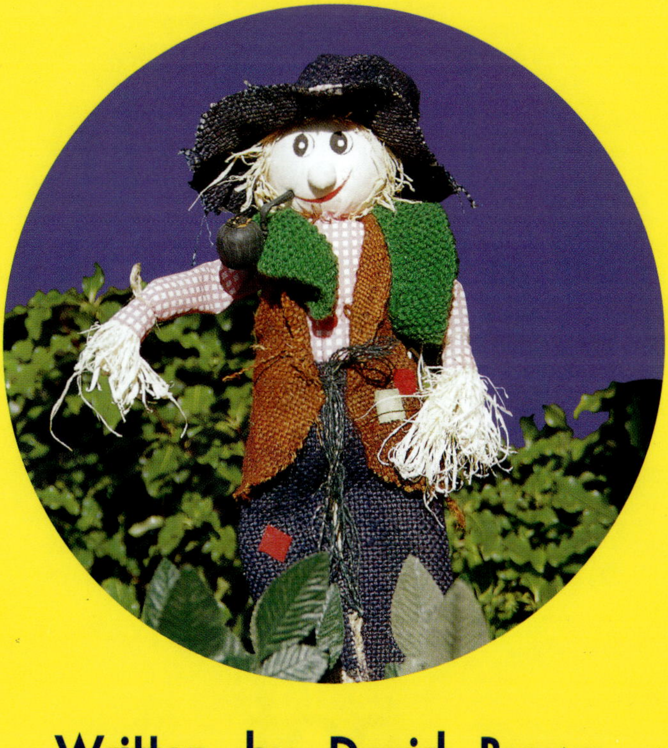

Written by David Brown

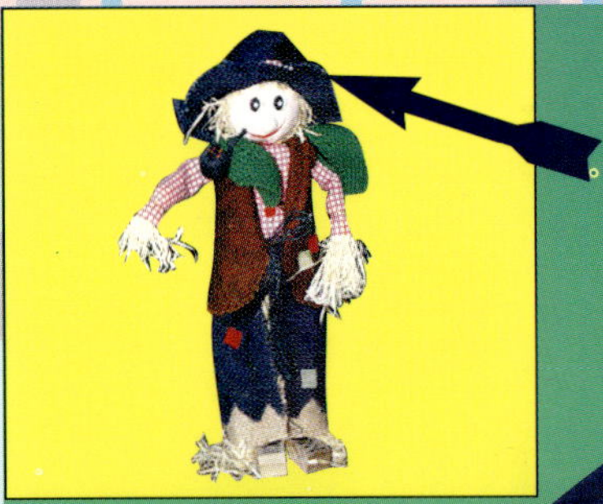

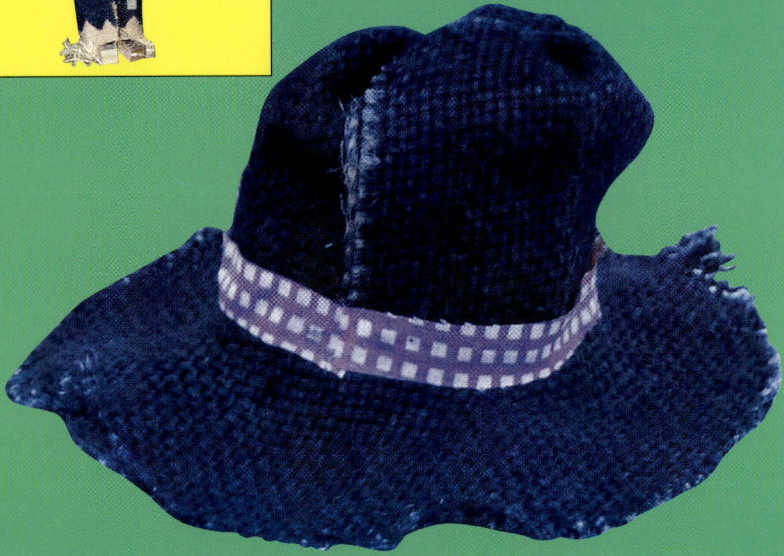

hat

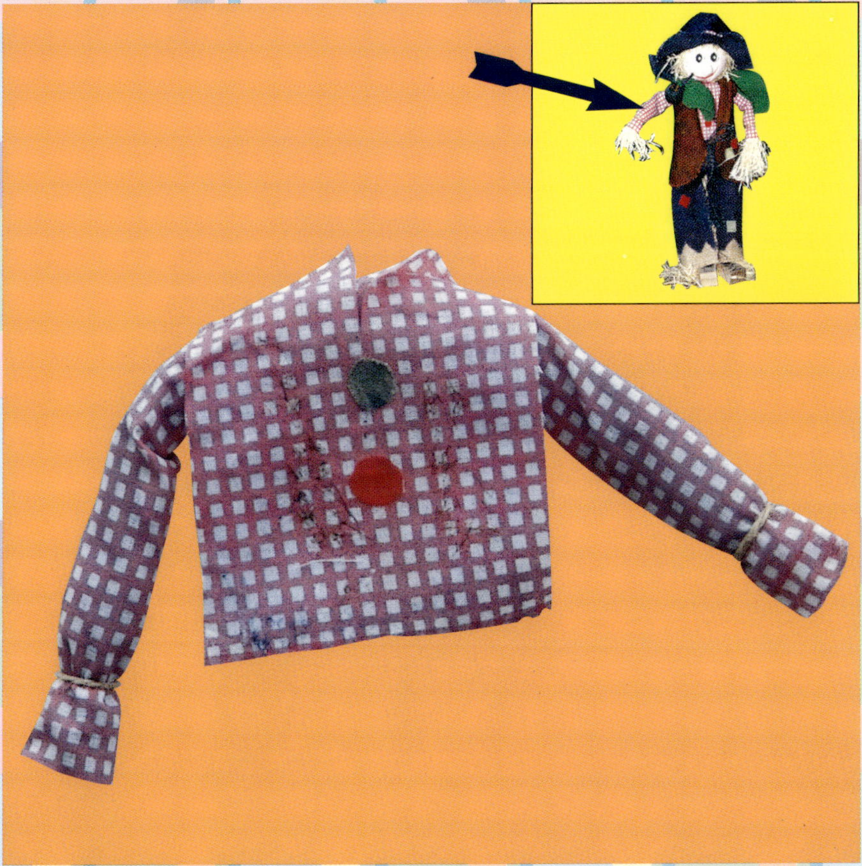

shirt

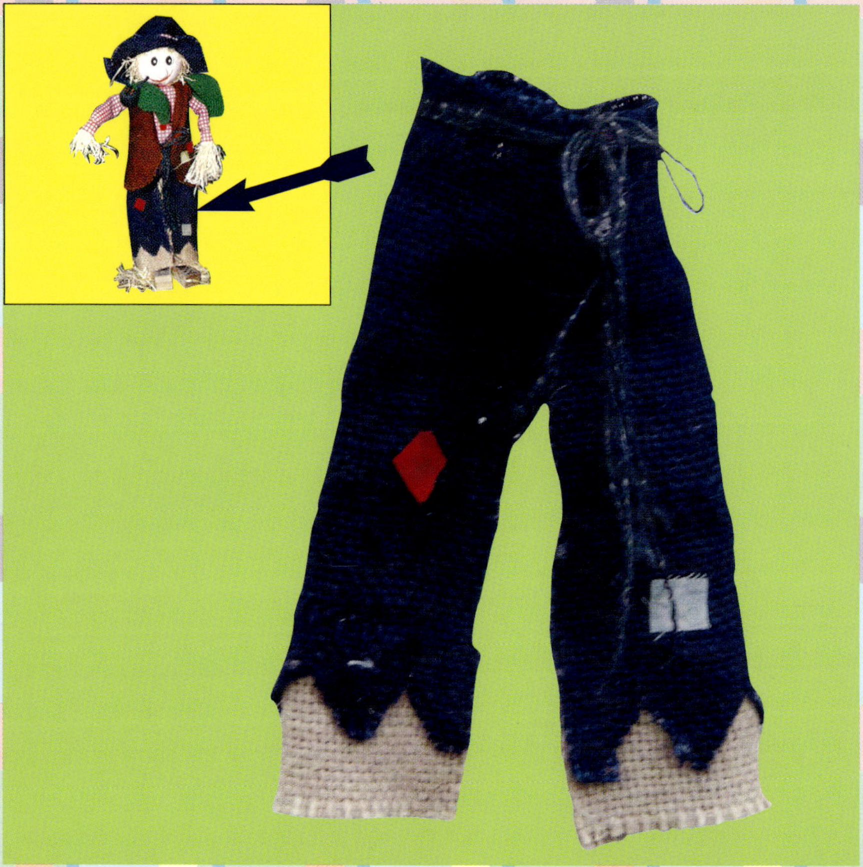

pants

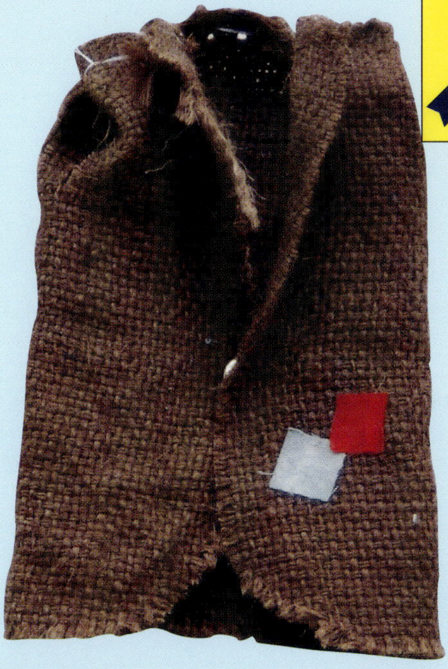

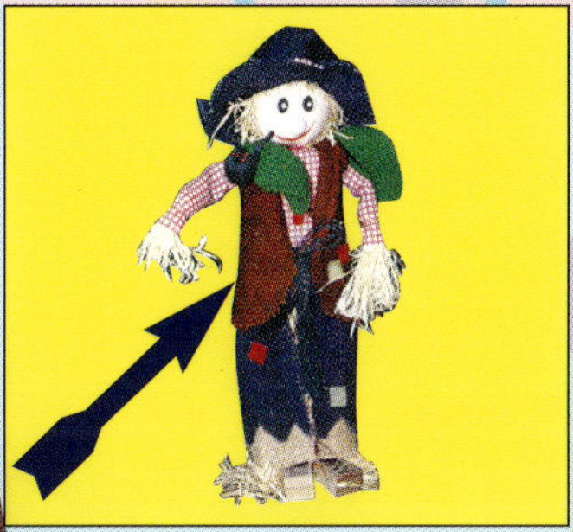

jacket

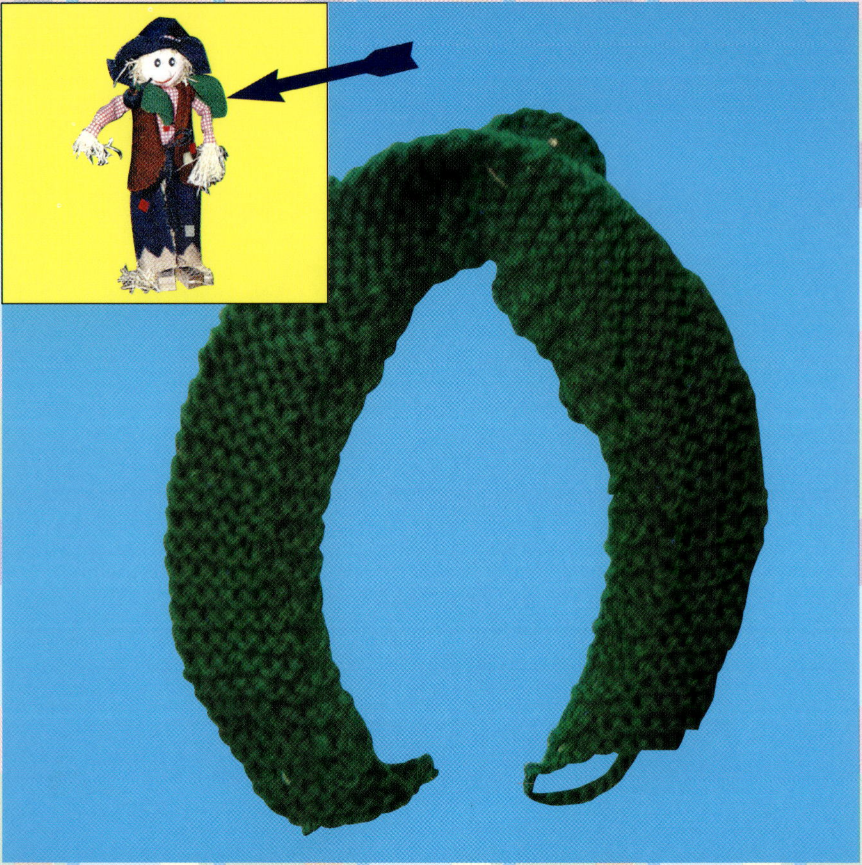

scarf

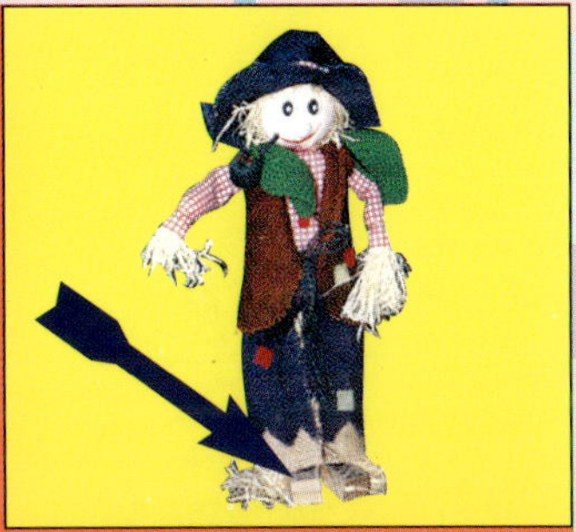

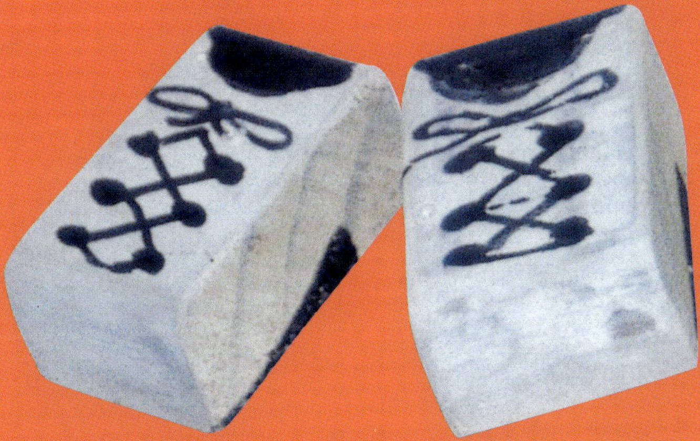

shoes

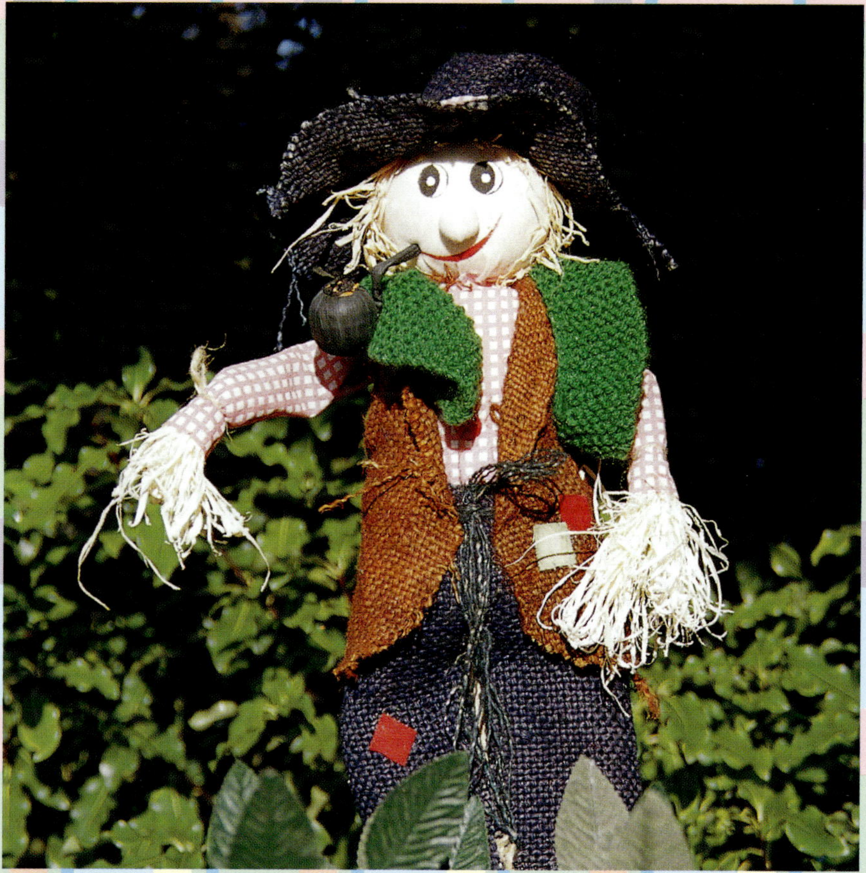

scarecrow